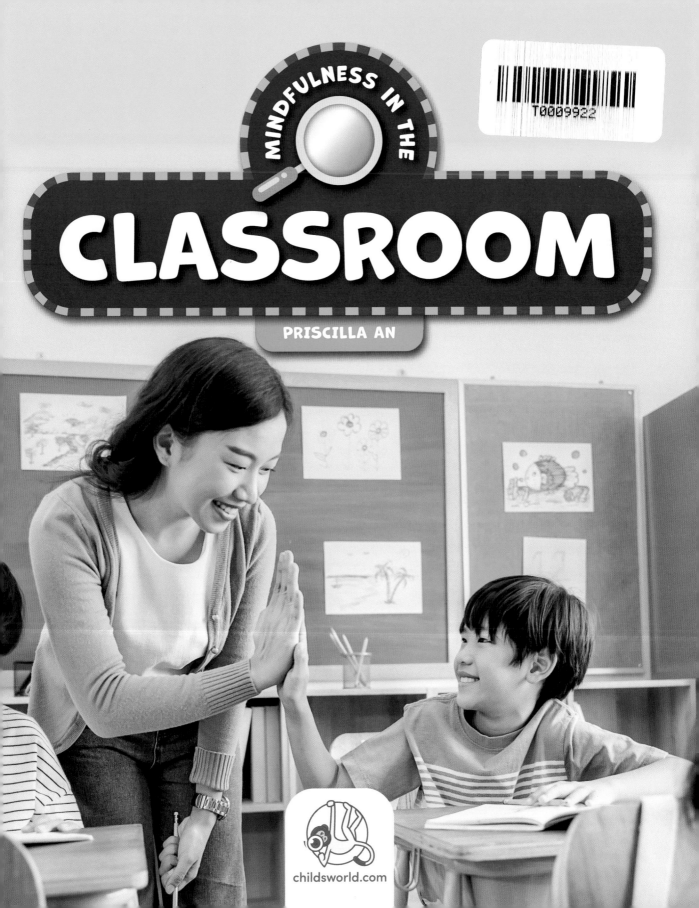

MINDFULNESS IN THE
CLASSROOM

PRISCILLA AN

childsworld.com

childsworld.com

Published by The Child's World®
800-599-READ · www.childsworld.com

Photography Credits
Photographs ©: Paula Photo/iStockphoto, cover, 1, 6–7, 13;
Rimma Bondarenko/Shutterstock Images, 3; iStockphoto,
5, 14–15, 16, 19, 20; Shutterstock Images, 8, 11, 22

ISBN Information
9781503869578 (Reinforced Library Binding)
9781503880887 (Portable Document Format)
9781503882195 (Online Multi-user eBook)
9781503883505 (Electronic Publication)
9781645498636 (Paperback)

LCCN 2022951198

Printed in the United States of America

Priscilla An is a children's book editor and author. She lives in Minnesota with her rabbit and likes to practice mindfulness through yoga.

TABLE OF CONTENTS

CHAPTER 1

WHAT IS MINDFULNESS? 4

CHAPTER 2

THOUGHT BUBBLES 6

CHAPTER 3

WHAT IF? 14

Wonder More . . . 21

Sitting Meditation . . . 22

Glossary . . . 23

Find Out More . . . 24

Index . . . 24

WHAT IS MINDFULNESS?

Sometimes students get **stressed** or upset at school. When this happens, their minds can **dwell** on whatever upset them. It might become hard to **focus** on schoolwork. Mindfulness can help. Mindfulness is when people are aware of their thoughts, feelings, and surroundings. Being mindful can help a person make good choices. Sometimes people experience negative emotions in the classroom. Mindfulness can help them react positively.

Mindfulness can help people focus on their feelings.

THOUGHT BUBBLES

Mark's class is learning how to subtract numbers. Ms. Chang writes out a math problem on the board. She asks the class to solve the problem.

Mark writes down the problem. He tries to follow what Ms. Chang taught. But he feels confused. He does not understand how to solve the problem.

Math can be hard to understand.

Many people experience stress at school.

WHAT IS STRESS?

Stress is a feeling that comes up when people are worried and frustrated about something. When someone is stressed, it can be hard to focus in the classroom. Stress can even cause stomachaches or headaches. Feeling stressed is a sign that a person needs to take a break. Students can take a break by getting a drink of water or taking a couple minutes to focus on their breathing.

The numbers start to look blurry. Mark looks around the classroom. It seems like everyone else knows how to solve the problem. He was already having a hard time with math. Now, he feels like he is going to fail the class. Mark puts his head down.

Ms. Chang walks over to Mark's desk. "Hey, Mark," she says. "Are you feeling OK?"

Mark shakes his head. "I can't understand this. It makes my head hurt. I will never understand, and I will fail this class!"

"We just learned this today!" Ms. Chang says. "It's OK if you do not understand it right away. You will have lots of time to practice. But it can be hard to practice when you are so worried about the future. We can try to get rid of some of those negative thoughts."

Mark scrunches his nose. "How do I do that?"

Ms. Chang smiles. "Well, sometimes I close my eyes, and I imagine my negative thoughts as bubbles. Then, I take a deep breath and blow the bubbles away. This helps me replace those negative thoughts with positive ones. Would you like to try that with me?"

Teachers are good sources of help.

Mark nods. He closes his eyes. He imagines his thoughts floating in the air. There is a bubble with a thought about failing the class. Another bubble is about not understanding anything. He takes a deep breath and slowly blows out. He imagines the two thought bubbles going far away until they pop.

Mark opens his eyes. His mind feels less crowded. He feels calmer. When Ms. Chang explains the math problem, Mark is able to focus. He begins to understand how to solve the problem.

Mindfulness can help people feel calmer.

Using his imagination to blow his negative thoughts away helped Mark clear his mind. Instead of being stressed about the future, Mark was able to focus on the present. Because he practiced mindfulness, Mark now feels in control of his thoughts.

WHAT IF?

Mr. Martinez's class had taken a big grammar test yesterday. Many students studied hard. Kaylin did not study very much. She felt like she understood everything really well. She also had done well in her practice test. Now Kaylin is excited to get her test back. She is sure that she got a good score.

Mr. Martinez begins handing back tests. When Kaylin's classmate Connor gets his test back, he jumps happily. "Yes! I got them all right!"

Studying for tests can be hard.

Getting a low score can make people sad.

It is now Kaylin's turn. She flips over the paper, expecting a score like Connor's. But she sees a 6/10 on the top of her test. Her heart drops. Tears start to form in her eyes. She feels like a failure.

Kaylin wishes she could turn back time. What would have happened if she had studied more? What if she had done one more practice problem? What if she had asked Mr. Martinez for more help?

Negative thoughts keep swirling in Kaylin's mind. These thoughts feel **overwhelming**. Kaylin needs to quiet her mind so she can think. She closes her eyes and breathes in slowly. Kaylin feels her stomach expand. She breathes out. Kaylin's shoulders relax.

Kaylin tells herself that she cannot change the past. Time travel does not happen in real life. Even though she did not get a perfect score, Kaylin still learned a lot. One low test score does not mean she is a failure. She can study the problems she got wrong to improve next time. As she takes each breath, Kaylin's mind feels a little lighter.

Kaylin hears her friend Olivia sigh. Olivia sits in front of Kaylin. She lowers her head and crinkles her test paper. Maybe she got a low score too. Kaylin thinks having someone to study with would be helpful.

"Olivia," Kaylin says. "Do you want to study together? I didn't do so well on my test."

Olivia turns around. Her face brightens. "I would love that!"

I AM NOT A FAILURE

Everyone experiences failure. People might not reach the goals they set. A person might finish a race in last place. But failures do not define a person. Instead of saying "I am a failure," people can say "I am enough."

Studying with friends can be helpful.

Thinking positive thoughts can change a person's mindset.

As class continues, Kaylin feels a lot better. She is still sad about her grade. But Kaylin knows she is not a failure. She can take a step forward. She even has a friend to study with. Kaylin is **confident** she can learn from her mistakes. She can try for a better grade next time.

WONDER MORE

Wondering about New Information

How much did you know about mindfulness before reading this book? What new information did you learn? Write down three new facts that this book taught you. Was the new information surprising? Why or why not?

Wondering How It Matters

What is one way being mindful in the classroom relates to your life? How do you think being mindful in the classroom relates to other kids' lives?

Wondering Why

Practicing mindfulness can help people's minds feel less crowded when they are stressed or overwhelmed. Why do you think it is important to clear your mind when you are stressed or overwhelmed? How might knowing this affect your life?

Ways to Keep Wondering

Learning about mindfulness in the classroom can be a complex topic. After reading this book, what questions do you have about it? What can you do to learn more about mindfulness?

SITTING MEDITATION

You can practice this sitting meditation if you feel stressed or overwhelmed.

1. Sit in your chair or any comfortable place in the classroom.

2. Close your eyes.

3. Breathe in slowly for three seconds. Think of the negative thoughts or emotions you are having.

4. Breathe out slowly for three seconds. Imagine that you are releasing all the negative thoughts.

5. Repeat a few times until you feel calmer.

6. To end the meditation, think of a positive thing to say. Try "I am enough" or "It is OK to ask for help."

GLOSSARY

confident (KON-fih-dent) When someone feels confident about something, she is certain about it. Kaylin feels confident that she can get a better test score next time.

define (deh-FYNE) To define is to make up the main qualities of something. Failure does not define who a person is.

dwell (DWELL) When people dwell on something, they think about it for a long time. Stress at school can make people dwell on negative thoughts, which makes it hard to think positively.

focus (FOH-kuss) To focus is to pay special attention to something. Stress can make it hard to focus on schoolwork.

frustrated (FRUH-stray-ted) To be frustrated is to be annoyed or angry. Mark was frustrated when he did not understand the math problem.

overwhelming (oh-vur-WELL-ming) When a thought or feeling becomes too much to handle, it can be overwhelming. Kaylin's thoughts felt overwhelming when she was thinking too much about her test score.

stressed (STREST) A person who is stressed feels pressured or worried. Mark felt very stressed when he thought he might fail his class.

FIND OUT MORE

In the Library

Anthony, William. *Mindfulness*. Minneapolis, MN: Bearport Publishing, 2021.

Krekelberg, Alyssa. *When Things Get Tough: Overcoming Obstacles*. Parker, CO: The Child's World, 2021.

Verde, Susan. *I Am Peace: A Book of Mindfulness*. New York, NY: Abrams, 2017.

On the Web

Visit our website for links about mindfulness in the classroom:

childsworld.com/links

Note to Parents, Caregivers, Teachers, and Librarians: We routinely verify our Web links to make sure they are safe and active sites. So encourage your readers to check them out!

INDEX

asking for help, 9–10, 17, 18

breathing, 8, 10–12, 17–18

failure, 9, 12, 17–20
focus, 4, 8, 12–13

grammar, 14

math, 6–9, 12
mindfulness exercises, 10–13, 17–18

practice, 10, 14, 17

stress, 4, 8, 13
studying, 14, 18–20

tests, 14–20